HOW TO USE THIS AWESOME BOOK

The next 4 pages are SAMPLE PAGES.

Copy the word at the top of the page on each line 1-9.

Each time you write the word, make it better and better each time!

Each day, write a new word 8 times using the dotted lines,
then on the 9th time, write it WITHOUT the dotted lines.

You will do EXCELLENT WORK!

Every 5th day, you will do a review of your AWESOME work,
writing all of the words from the last 4 days in sentences.

I made this book to write a new word each day Monday (blue), Tuesday (orange),
Wednesday (purple) and Thursday (green), then reviewing the words and writing
sentences on Friday (the next page).

YOU ARE AWESOME!

Design by April Chloe Terrazas | © 2016 Crazy Brainz, LLC | www.AprilChloeTerrazasAmazon.com
No portion of this book may be reproduced without express written consent from April Chloe Terrazas.
ISBN#: 978-1-941775-34-9

Sample Page

B a k e	L a k e
1. Bake	Lake
2. Bake	Lake
3. Bake	Lake
4. Bake	Lake
5. Bake	Lake
6. Bake	Lake
7. Bake	Lake
8. Bake	Lake
9. Write the word without the lines Bake	Write the word without the lines Lake
You are AMAZING!	Good Job!

Sample Page

Make	Take
1. Make	Take
2. Make	Take
3. Make	Take
4. Make	Take
5. Make	Take
6. Make	Take
7. Make	Take
8. Make	Take
9. Write the word without the lines Make	Write the word without the lines Take
You are AMAZING!	*Good Job!*

Sample Page

Drawing Space

Practice reading and writing the sentences

They bake a cake.

They bake a cake.

The lake has water.

The lake has water.

I make a cake.

I make a cake.

I take the cake.

I take the cake.

Sample Page

Practice Writing Each Word

Bake

Bake
Bake Bake
Bake
Bake
Bake Bake
Bake Bake

Lake

Lake
Lake
Lake
Lake
Lake
Lake
Lake

Make

Make
Make
Make
Make

Make

Take

Take
Take Take
Take Take
Take
Take

Bake	Lake

1.

2.

3.

4.

5.

6.

7.

8.

9. Write the word without the lines | Write the word without the lines

|

Wednesday	Tuesday
Make	Take

1.

2.

3.

4.

5.

6.

7.

8.

9. Write the word without the lines | Write the word without the lines

You are AMAZING! | *Good Job!*

Drawing Space

Practice reading and writing the sentences

They bake a cake.

The lake has water.

I make a cake.

I take the cake.

Practice Writing Each Word

Bake	Lake
Make	Take

Monday	Tuesday
M o m	**D a d**

1.

2.

3.

4.

5.

6.

7.

8.

9.

Write the word without the lines	Write the word without the lines

| *You are AMAZING!* | *Good Job!* |

Girl	Boy
1.	
2.	
3.	
4.	
5.	
6.	
7.	
8.	
9. Write the word without the lines	Write the word without the lines
You are AMAZING!	*Good Job!*

Drawing Space

Practice reading and writing the sentences

My mom is nice.

My dad is nice.

The girl likes to play.

The boy likes to play.

Practice Writing Each Word

Mom	Dad

Girl	Boy

Monday	Tuesday
E a t	**M e a t**

1.

2.

3.

4.

5.

6.

7.

8.

9. Write the word without the lines | Write the word without the lines

You are AMAZING! | *Good Job!*

Seat	Heat

1.

2.

3.

4.

5.

6.

7.

8.

9. Write the word without the lines | Write the word without the lines

You are AMAZING! | *Good Job!*

Drawing Space

Practice reading and writing the sentences

I   eat   a   taco.

The   taco   has   meat.

Sit   in   your   seat.

I   like   summer   heat.

Practice Writing Each Word

Eat	Meat

Seat	Heat

B e e	**S e e**

1.

2.

3.

4.

5.

6.

7.

8.

9. Write the word without the lines | Write the word without the lines

You are AMAZING! | *Good Job!*

Wednesday	Tuesday
F e e	T h r e e

1.

2.

3.

4.

5.

6.

7.

8.

9.

Write the word without the lines	Write the word without the lines
You are AMAZING!	*Good Job!*

Friday

Drawing Space

Practice reading and writing the sentences

The bee is small.

I see the bee.

The fee is $1.00.

I see three bees.

Practice Writing Each Word

Bee	See

Fee	Three

C o w	N o w

1.

2.

3.

4.

5.

6.

7.

8.

9. Write the word without the lines | Write the word without the lines

You are AMAZING!   *Good Job!*

Wednesday	Tuesday
W o w	**H o w**

1.

2.

3.

4.

5.

6.

7.

8.

9. Write the word without the lines | Write the word without the lines

You are AMAZING! | *Good Job!*

Drawing Space

Practice reading and writing the sentences

The cow was small.

Now the cow is big.

Wow the cow is big.

How big is the cow?

Practice Writing Each Word

Cow	Now

Wow	How

His	Her

1.

2.

3.

4.

5.

6.

7.

8.

9. Write the word without the lines | Write the word without the lines

You are AMAZING! | *Good Job!*

Wednesday	Tuesday
Your	Mine

1.

2.

3.

4.

5.

6.

7.

8.

9. Write the word without the lines | Write the word without the lines

You are AMAZING! | *Good Job!*

Friday

Drawing Space

Practice reading and writing the sentences

The toy is his.

Her friend is nice.

Your friend is nice.

The toy is mine.

Practice Writing Each Word

His	Her

Your	Mine

Cat	Dog

1.

2.

3.

4.

5.

6.

7.

8.

9. Write the word without the lines   Write the word without the lines

You are AMAZING!   *Good Job!*

Bird	Duck

1.

2.

3.

4.

5.

6.

7.

8.

9. Write the word without the lines | Write the word without the lines

You are AMAZING! | Good Job!

Friday

Drawing Space

Practice reading and writing the sentences

The cat is cute.

The dog is cute.

The bird is purple.

The duck is green.

Practice Writing Each Word

Cat	Dog

Bird	Duck

Cat

C a r	T r u c k

1.

2.

3.

4.

5.

6.

7.

8.

9. | Write the word without the lines | Write the word without the lines |

| You are AMAZING! | Good Job! |

Wednesday	Tuesday
B u s	**B o a t**

1.

2.

3.

4.

5.

6.

7.

8.

9. Write the word without the lines | Write the word without the lines

You are AMAZING! | *Good Job!*

Friday

Drawing Space

Practice reading and writing the sentences

The car is fast.

The truck is slow.

The bus is big.

The boat floats.

Practice Writing Each Word

Car	Truck

Bus	Boat

	A n d	B a n d
1.		
2.		
3.		
4.		
5.		
6.		
7.		
8.		
9.	Write the word without the lines	Write the word without the lines
	You are AMAZING!	*Good Job!*

H a n d	L a n d

1.

2.

3.

4.

5.

6.

7.

8.

9. Write the word without the lines | Write the word without the lines

You are AMAZING! | *Good Job!*

Friday

Drawing Space

Practice reading and writing the sentences

She and I eat cake.

The band is loud.

My hand is small.

The land is green.

Practice Writing Each Word

And	Band

Hand	Land

Best	Rest

1.

2.

3.

4.

5.

6.

7.

8.

9. Write the word without the lines | Write the word without the lines

You are AMAZING!   *Good Job!*

Test	West

1.

2.

3.

4.

5.

6.

7.

8.

9. Write the word without the lines | Write the word without the lines

You are AMAZING! | *Good Job!*

Friday

Drawing Space

Practice reading and writing the sentences

You are the best.

I want to rest.

My test was easy.

We are going west.

Practice Writing Each Word

Best	Rest

Test	West

Monday	Tuesday
A l l	B a l l

1.

2.

3.

4.

5.

6.

7.

8.

9. Write the word without the lines | Write the word without the lines

You are AMAZING! | *Good Job!*

Call	Tall

1.

2.

3.

4.

5.

6.

7.

8.

9. Write the word without the lines | Write the word without the lines

You are AMAZING! | *Good Job!*

Friday

Drawing Space

Practice reading and writing the sentences

We are all going.

I want to play ball.

We call our friend.

We are growing tall.

Practice Writing Each Word

All	Ball

Call	Tall

All | Ball

Cold	Hold

1.

2.

3.

4.

5.

6.

7.

8.

9. Write the word without the lines | Write the word without the lines

You are AMAZING! | *Good Job!*

Sold   Told

1.

2.

3.

4.

5.

6.

7.

8.

9. Write the word without the lines   Write the word without the lines

You are AMAZING!   *Good Job!*

Drawing Space

Practice reading and writing the sentences

We   are   cold.

Please   hold   the   baby.

We   sold   our   house.

He told me about the party.

Practice Writing Each Word

Cold	Hold

Sold	Told

www.ingramcontent.com/pod-product-compliance
Lightning Source LLC
Chambersburg PA
CBHW042359030426
42337CB00032B/5156